HISTORY OF WATER COLOR PAINTING IN AMERICA

HISTORY OF WATER COLOR PAINTING IN AMERICA

Albert Ten Eyck Gardner

Reinhold Publishing Corporation/New York

Acknowledgements

The author wishes especially to thank his colleagues at The Metropolitan Museum of Art, Mr. Stuart P. Feld, Mrs. Suzanne K. Nelson, and Mr. James Humphrey, for their criticisms and cooperation. I am also indebted to the librarians of the New York Society Library, Miss Sylvia Hilton and Miss Helen Ruskell, to Miss Caroline Scoon of The New-York Historical Society, Miss Grace Mayer and Mr. Richard Tooke of The Museum of Modern Art, Miss Margaret McKellar of the Whitney Museum of American Art, Mr. Axel von Saldern and Mr. Donelson Hoopes of The Brooklyn Museum, Mr. E. L. Kallup of The Cooper Union Museum, Miss Elizabeth E. Roth and Mr. Willson Duprey of the Print Room and Miss Jean MacNiece of the Manuscript Room of The New York Public Library, and Mr. Albert Baragwanath of the Museum of the City of New York.

Contents

Introduction

WATER COLOR IN SOME FORM HAS BEEN USED BY ARTISTS since prehistoric times and in all parts of the world. Usually, in Europe, the early types of water color pigment produced opaque colors. The technological advances in paint manufacture and in paper making that developed in England in the last decades of the eighteenth century enabled and encouraged British artists to develop their technique of painting with transparent colors on specially made white paper.

This is not to imply that earlier European artists did not use water colors for the production of finished pictures. Good examples, for instance, will be found in the work of Albrecht Dürer (1471-1528).

Although water colors are usually given to beginners to work with, the medium is one of the most challenging and difficult to handle. It requires a quick, sure hand, trained by constant practice, and demands a skill far beyond that of the average student. Yet in the controlled hand of an expert, the most beautiful effects can be obtained. Water color has always had a special appeal to women, and throughout the nineteenth century hundreds of feminine artists produced their often charming landscapes, flower studies, and sketches of autumn leaves. Among the professional women artists, one of the most successful was the Boston painter Ellen Robbins, whose still-life pictures of American wild flowers are painted in a most accomplished manner.

Although water color painting has always been used by European artists, the art as we know it today did not begin to develop until the end of the eighteenth century. Many American artists worked in water color throughout the nineteenth century, but almost all of them continued to paint in oil and most of them were much better known for their oil paintings than for their water colors. This has always been true, and it makes it difficult to consider American water color painting as a subject apart from the general history of painting. In fact, water color painting in America usually followed the changes in style and choice of subject to be found in oil painting.

Water color, because of its flexible character and many uses, does not lend itself to the usual kind of chronological historical treatment. The various modes of using water color were all carried on simultaneously for a very long time — from the middle of the eighteenth century to the present, in fact. In general, it may be said that until modern times very few American artists confined themselves exclusively to water color as did so many British artists of the nineteenth century.

In this country the art of water color painting began by following closely upon British precedent. In the closing years of the eighteenth century and for the first half of the nineteenth century, no prominent artists in America devoted themselves solely to the medium, and many of the productions of this early period came from the hands of primitive painters and amateurs and those few professional artists who came from England to settle in this country.

The development of water color painting in America cannot be explained or properly understood without some account of the remarkable flourishing of the art in England in the last decades of the eighteenth century and in the early years of the nineteenth century. In some respects water color painting, especially the painting of landscapes, might be considered as an almost exclusive British monopoly. At that time the principal impetus, inspiration, and influences on American water color painting came entirely from English sources. But later, after the Civil War, when American art students began to flock to Paris, French and other European factors began to have their influence.

The development of water color landscape painting in England in the eighteenth century was closely associated with print making. To satisfy the increased demand for colored prints artists were engaged by print sellers to paint topographical views in water color of the country houses of the nobility and ruined castles and abbeys. These drawings were then reproduced as engravings or as aquatints. The great demand for hand-colored prints caused some print sellers to hire young artists to give the prints washes of color. Many of the most famous English water color painters started their careers in this humble occupation — among them Girtin and Turner. The change from the eighteenth-century "stained drawing" to the free, transparent water color painting, came about very gradually and was the result of innovations in technique introduced by the British landscape painters Sandby, Girtin, Cozzens, and Cotman. It reached its highest development in the work of Turner in the first half of the nineteenth century.

Perhaps the strongest influence which encouraged water color landscape painting in the later eighteenth century in England and America was the change in attitude towards the natural landscape itself. In the early eighteenth century wild alpine crags and rough mountainous country were generally considered as horrid places to be shunned — mere impediments to the traveller. But as the century advanced there was a remarkable change in this attitude. Interest became active in the so-called English garden, where trees, shrubs and flowers, lawns and meadows were laid out to look as though planted accidentally by nature. From interest in this kind of garden there arose a wider appreciation of nature extending even to landscapes of the wildest kind. There is a passage in Southey's *Letters from England* (1807) which reflects this change in attitude. He wrote: "Within the last thirty years a taste for the picturesque has sprung up; — and a course of summer travel is now looked upon to be as essential as ever a course of spring physic was in old times . . . to confess the truth, I have myself caught something of this passion for the picturesque, from conversations, from

books, and still more from the beautiful landscapes in water colours, in which the English excel all other nations."

Since water color materials are easily transported and can be used out-of-doors, most of the British landscape painters developed a taste for painting direct from nature. Some wealthy travellers hired professional artists to go along with them to record the views and monuments of the journey. Other artists, travelling on their own, recorded picturesque views in water color that were later reproduced as aquatints and sold in portfolios or bound as books.

A curious event that is said to have turned the attention of British artists to painting picturesque views of famous castles, country houses, monastic ruins, and ancient monuments was the commissioning of Josiah Wedgwood by the Russian Empress Catherine the Great to produce a dinner and dessert service of between 1200 and 2000 pieces, each to be decorated with a different English landscape. Wedgwood's efforts to round up engravings and water colors received some publicity, and he hired artists to travel about England and Scotland to paint views especially to be copied by china painters on this tremendous set of dishes. This famous service was exhibited in London in 1774 before being shipped to Russia.

One often overlooked factor in the rapid rise in the popularity of water color painting in England and America was the development of the commercial production of especially prepared colors and papers manufactured for the use of artists. In early times painters had to buy their raw pigments from an apothecary or herbalist and grind their own colors. The commercial production of pans or cakes of water color was first started by Thomas and William Reeves in London, about 1780. The good quality of their colors won for them a silver palette awarded by the Royal Society of Arts in 1781. By 1783, Reeves water colors were imported from England and offered for sale in New York, but, because of tariffs and taxes, they were expensive. The first successful commercial manufacture of artists' colors in America was developed by G. W. Osborne in Philadelphia, where his water colors were shown at the first exhibition of the Franklin Institute in 1824. The following year a box of his colors was awarded a medal by the Institute. He advertised his colors as "Osborne's Superfine American Water Colors, Warranted Equal to Any Imported." His colors won the approval of the artists Thomas Sully, Samuel F. B. Morse and Titian Peale. About 1832 the British firm of artists' colormen Winsor & Newton began to produce water color paint in the form of a moist paste in collapsable metal tubes. From the time of Reeves onward there were many improvements made in the manufacture of water color paint as the knowledge of paint chemistry increased during the nineteenth century.

In the last years of the eighteenth century, the paper-making industry was greatly expanded in England, and about 1775 the firm of Whatman began making paper especially designed for water color painting. Papers were also made to the demands and specifications of individual artists, and many improvements in manufacture were effected. The first paper mill in the Colonies was that of William Rittenhouse, who began to make paper about 1690 near Philadelphia on a little stream still known as Papermill Run. Whether the Rittenhouse mill ever produced paper especially for the use of artists is not known, but throughout the eighteenth century Philadelphia remained one of the most important paper-making centers in the country.

Influences from the British art world were introduced to American art circles by native artists who returned home from study with Benjamin West, the American painter who, in 1792, became president of the Royal Academy in London. But perhaps more important were the British or British-trained Irish artists who came to settle in this country. James Cox arrived about 1790 and opened a drawing academy; William Birch and Hugh Bridport came in 1794; John Barralet, a Dublin trained painter, came in 1796; William Haines in 1802; William Bennett and

John Hill in 1816; Joshua Shaw in 1817, and William G. Wall in 1818. Wall produced a series of water color views of the Hudson Valley and published and sold colored aquatints reproducing the original drawings. This was called the *Hudson River Portfolio*, put out in two editions, in 1820 and in 1828. This followed the custom of the British artists who published their views of the English lakes, the Scottish highlands, and ancient castles. The twenty hand-colored prints in Wall's *Hudson River Portfolio* are said to be the finest collection of New York State views ever published. These prints were often copied in water color by students, amateurs, and professional artists. They were influential in directing the attention of American artists to the scenic beauties of the Hudson Valley.

Two other English immigrant artists collaborated on the production of a portfolio, *Picturesque Views of American Scenery*, published in Philadelphia in 1820. The water color drawings were made by Joshua Shaw and reproduced in aquatint by John Hill. A printed statement on the inside of the cover of the second part of this series reads: "Our country abounds with Scenery, comprehending all varieties of the Sublime, the beautiful, and the picturesque in nature, worthy to engage the skill of an artist in their delineation. . . . Mr. Shaw, whose merits in this line have been honored with the commendation of Mr. West, is travelling through the different States, for the purpose of taking, on the spot, the best and most popular Views."

The commercial manufacture of artists' colors, papers, and brushes which developed in the United States in the 1820's placed the materials of the art of water color painting within the reach of many aspiring artists. In addition to the demand for artists' materials, there arose a demand for drawing books and books of instruction in painting. At first, American publishers issued reprints of British books of this sort. These drawing books were illustrated with simple landscapes for the student to copy or to add color to. However, the English books were illustrated with views of castles and thatched cottages such as no American child or young art student was familiar with.

The number of drawing books and manuals for the instruction of painters published in this country from Colonial times down through the nineteenth century is unexpectedly large. Though the early ones were, of course, pirated reprints of English books, American drawing teachers soon began compiling their own books and illustrating them with American subjects. One of the earliest of these was Archibald Robertson's *Elements of Graphic Art*, published in 1802, but the most handsomely illustrated one was *The Art of Colouring and Painting Landscapes*, the work of Fielding Lucas, issued in Baltimore in 1815 and later. His books were illustrated with beautifully drawn views of American scenery reproduced in aquatint from original water colors.

One of the prime influences in spreading a knowledge of water color painting in America was the drawing master, who offered to train young ladies and gentlemen in the art. One of the earliest of these was William Burgis, the engraver, whose views of New York, Boston, and Harvard College are among the rarest early American prints. In December, 1733, Mrs. Jacob Franks, the mother of one of his pupils in New York, wrote to her son in England: "Your brother Moses intends to send Farinelli back again done upon glass, which way of painting he does very well as he also does in Indian ink. Several gentlemen that understand drawing say he will do mighty well in time — his master Mr. Burgis says he never met with anyone that took the outlines of any so true and in so little time as he will. . . ."*

Through the later years of the eighteenth century other drawing masters appeared in the Colonies. Among the more prominent ones, besides Cox, was the miniature painter Archibald Robertson, a Scot, who settled in New York in 1791 and with his brother Alexander conducted for many years an art school called the Columbian Academy. The following advertisement, published by James Cox in the *Pennsyl-*

vania Packet, September 2, 1790, describes the kind of school in which water color painting was taught in the first decades of the nineteenth century: "The subscriber returns his grateful acknowledgments to his Friends and the generous Public, for the liberal patronage he has received, and begs leave to inform them, that he has removed his School opposite to Mr. John Elliot's the Bank side of Front Street, below Chestnut street — Where he continues Instructing Youth in the useful and elegant Accomplishments of Drawing and Painting, upon Paper, Glass, Canvas, Muslin, and Sattin; also, Shading with India Ink. Those ladies and gentlemen who please to honor him with the tuition of their children, may rest assured that no effort shall be wanting on his part to to give general satisfaction. Coats of Arms neatly drawn and painted; Pictures framed, glaized and gilded, in the most elegant and modern style; superfine colors and India Ink prepared, and warranted superior to any imported. Copperplate Prints, Maps and Paintings, accurately copied; Drawing and Shading on Sattin for Needle-Work; likewise, Ladies or Gentlemen desirous of improving in any of the above Branches, will be waited upon at their own apartments, on the most reasonable terms, by James Cox. N.B. Commands addressed to him at his School, or at Mr. Peale's Museum, will be punctually attended to."

Although some drawing and water color painting was taught in the regular schools, the subject did not become a serious study until the middle of the nineteenth century.

In the 1840's the work of the British painter Turner began to have an effect on American water color painting. Knowledge of Turner's painting was introduced by the writings of John Ruskin, principally through his book *Modern Painters: their superiority in the art of landscape painting to all the Ancient Masters proved by examples of the True, the Beautiful, and the Intellectual, from the works of modern artists, especially those of J. M. W. Turner, Esq., R.A.* This book was published in 1843. It became one of the most important influences on

* From a letter in the collection of the American Jewish Historical Society, New York.

American art in general and on American attitudes toward art in the second half of the nineteenth century. John Durand, in his biography of his father Asher B. Durand, the painter, says of this influence: "It must be stated here that at this time the public mind in America had been quickened in relation to art by the writings and teachings of Mr. Ruskin. Whatever may be said of the criticisms of works of art . . . by this eminent writer . . . of his theories, hobbies and idiosyncracies, it is certain that he developed more interest in art in the United States than all other agencies put together. His remarkable word painting, the theological bent of his mind, his ascetic temperament . . . furnished both pulpit and press with material for sermons, news and gossip about art . . . and spread a knowledge of art among people who would not otherwise have given it a thought."

Turner's use of brilliant colors made many artists discard their brown paint; and his bold, broad manner of painting landscapes loosened the tight, meticulous technique that had until then been the general manner of the artists of the first generation of the Hudson River School of landscape painters. Asher B. Durand, in his book *Letters on Landscape Painting,* published in 1855, says of him: "Turner gathered from the previously unexplored sky, alone, transcripts of Nature whose mingled beauty of form and chiaroscuro have immortalized him, for the sole reason that he has therein approached nearer to the representation of the infinity of Nature than all that have gone before him."

In England in the middle decades of the nineteenth century the water color painters received much attention from Queen Victoria and the Prince Consort. The Queen purchased a great number of pictures from the annual exhibitions of the Watercolor Society in London. Additional interest in the art was aroused on both sides of the Atlantic when it was learned that she had been sketching in the Scottish Highlands under the instruction of the Prince Consort and Sir Edwin Landseer, the famous English animal painter.

One element that directed and sustained the interest of British artists in water color painting was the steady advance in the prices they were able to get for their pictures. The collectors of water colors bidding in competition for the works of popular artists drove the prices at auction up very high.

Many of the sciences and professions called upon the water color painter to give pictorial or diagrammatic form to the ideas of inventors, engineers, doctors, botanists, ornithologists and archaeologists. This aspect of water color painting is shown in the production of the so-called documentary picture. Of this type the best known is the topographical landscape, but other types are not to be overlooked, such as town and street views, architectural renderings of the facades of elevations of buildings, and mechanical drawings, which in the nineteenth century were often finished in water color. Another use of water color was for the preparation of illustrations for books on ornithology, botany, and medicine. Among the American works of this kind the ornithological water color drawings of John James Audubon are perhaps the most beautiful examples.

One of the most significant periods in the history of American water color painting was the decade 1850-1860, for in that time the American Society of Painters in Water Color was formed (1850). The first important exhibition organized by this group was shown in the New York Crystal Palace in 1853. Another important event was the large exhibition of British art shown in New York and Boston in the winter of 1857-1858. This consisted of three hundred oil paintings and two hundred water colors. The exhibition was notable for the full representation of the works of the Pre-Raphaelite artists and its large group of water colors, among them six landscapes by Turner and one study by Ruskin.

Another indication of the increased interest in water color in the 1850's was the publication in the *Bulletin of the American Art Union* of a series of articles titled "The Art of Landscape Painting in Water Colors" (beginning with the issue of November 1, 1851). These articles discussed the materials, methods, and techniques of water color painting in great detail. At that time the Art Union's *Bulletin* was distributed to its several thousand members in all parts of the country.

The formation of societies of water color painters both in London and in New York was prompted by the fact that these artists felt that their pictures did not show to advantage in the spaces allotted to them in exhibitions that were primarily made up of oil paintings. The division of oils and water colors into separate exhibitions was caused partly for aesthetic considerations, but the separation was also, at least in part, caused by economic considerations, as it was found that the sale of water colors was much reduced when both kinds of paintings were shown together. The best published account of the American Water Color Society appeared about thirty years after the Society was organized and after its regular annual exhibitions had become an accepted part of the New York art world. It appeared in the first volume of the *American Art Annual* of 1898. This informative account is reprinted here in its entirety.

"THE AMERICAN WATER COLOR SOCIETY
Board of Control, 1898-1899

J. G. Brown, President	J. Symington, Treasurer
C. Harry Eaton, Secretary, 53 E. 23d St.	C. D. Weldon
Irving R. Wiles	Walter Shirlaw
	Wm. J. Whittemore

A number of gentlemen, many of whom were designers and engravers, having satisfactorily experimented in the use of water colors, and still further encouraged by the success of the old London Society of Painters in Water Colors in affirmatively settling the long disputed question as to the durability of water color paintings, established a life school in New York for the development of the art in this country. From this on Christmas Day, 1850, emanated under an adopted constitution the first Society of Painters in Water Colors in America. Regular meetings were held in various places from time to time, when at length an amendment to the constitution was passed, providing for an annual public exhibition "to cultivate in the public a taste for the art." The result was that at the "Exhibition of the Industry of all Nations," held in the Crystal Palace, New York, in 1853, quite a collection of water colors was exhibited. These works were hung by themselves on screens, and were classed in the catalogue as "Water Color Paintings by Members of the New York Water Color Society." There is, however, no record of an "annual" exhibition held by the Society, and it may rightfully be inferred that it expended itself at its initial display, since it shortly thereafter passed out of existence.

With the exception of a few exhibitions of foreign subjects, nothing in the line of water colors was again publicly shown until in the autumn of 1866, when an organization called the Artists' Fund Society of New York made a feature of water color paintings in conjunction with the oil exhibition of the National Academy, which proved so popular that a nucleus of the old organization, augmented by others, met at Mr. Gilbert Burling's studio in the New York University Building on the evening of December 5th, 1866, and there formed themselves into the "American Society of Painters in Water Colors," which became incorporated eleven years after under the more euphonious title of the American Water Color Society.

The officers selected to guide the new venture were: Samuel Colman, President; Gilbert Burling, Secretary, and Mr. Rawson, Treasurer. The latter resigning, James D. Smillie took his place and held the office until elevated to the Presidency, serving in both capacities through a period of twelve years. The lay members were Alfred Fredericks, Frederick F. Durand, Edward Hooper, Constant Mayer, John M. Falconer, R. Swain Gifford, T. C. Nicoll, Harry Fenn, J. F. Cropsey, Marcus Waterman, Henry Van Ingen, Napoleon Sarony, T. C. Farar and Alexander Wust. Of these J. F. Cropsey, Alfred Fredericks and John M. Falconer had belonged to the original Society of Painters in Water Colors.

The new society opened its first exhibition on December 21st, 1867, in New York, at the National Academy of Design, where every winter since it has revealed to the public the progress made in the fascinating art it stands for.

The Society is indebted to the generosity of Mr. William T. Evans for a prize of $300, to be awarded by the Jury of Selection, for the most meritorious water color in the exhibition, painted in this country by an American artist, without limit to age; the recipient of the prize to be thereafter ineligible.

1888. Horatio Walker.	1893. Sarah C. Sears.
1889. George W. Maynard.	1894. J. Francis Murphy.
1890. Wm. T. Smedley.	1895. Walter L. Palmer.
1891. A. H. Wyant.	1896. W. L. Lathrop.
1892. C. Morgan McIlhenney.	1897. Irving R. Wiles.

1898. C. Harry Eaton."

The first president of the American Water Color Society, Samuel Colman (1832-1920), was one of the most interesting and prolific water color artists of his time. He was the son of a prosperous publisher and book seller in New York. Colman studied art with the landscape painter Asher B. Durand and in Paris, where he went in 1860. Although he is not well remembered today, he was a remarkable man with many interests. He was not only a painter but also a designer of interiors and, with Louis Tiffany, organizer of the Tiffany Studios. He was also a collector of Oriental porcelains. Isham, in *The History of American Painting*, says of Colman's water colors: "There was, in fact, much of

Colman's love of warm, pure color in his paintings in transparent wash or in gouache on rough straw board, of Italian or Mexican scenes that used to light up the early exhibitions of the Water Color Society, the firmness of outline and energy of drawing being probably the result of the French training."

In a foreword to the catalogue of the First Combined Exhibition of the New York Water Color Club and the American Water Color Society in the winter of 1921, Alphaeus Cole, then Secretary of the Exhibition Committee, gave an account of the early days of the Society and told something about the New York Water Color Club and how it happened to be organized. He wrote: "Those who are old enough to have memories of the happenings of fifty years ago will doubtless think, as they look at the water colors in the galleries of the Fine Arts Building, of the first exhibitions held by the American Water Color Society in Twenty-third Street. They will remember the eager enthusiasm of the public who waited in crowds outside anxious to be the first to enter when the doors opened, and fearful lest, when they did get in, there might be no unsold pictures left for them to purchase. 'Galt, Galt' they would cry on catching a glimpse of the familiar figure of the famous picture salesman, 'Be sure and give me first pick.' In those days the salesman made enough out of his commissions to take a trip to Europe, and the American Water Color Society was a flourishing institution which could afford to entertain its members and exhibitors in a style not yet forgotten.

"The annual smoker was awaited with eager anticipation by many a hungry artist whose picture had been accepted. Imagine the thrill the youngster got who ate and possibly smoked for the first time with men like William Chase, Alexander Wyant, or Hopkinson Smith. The refreshments are still talked of — 'Golly, what eats! Oyster-patties, chicken salad and cigars any amount. Why some fellows ate enough for a month.'"

There is an amusing story told of an artist of talent who was invited to contribute a picture to the annual exhibition, but who not being ready sent in an empty frame accompanied by a note to say the picture would follow.

The day before the opening he was warned that the committee could wait no longer. The artist had only been able to paint the sky, but perceiving that the white foreground looked like snow, he stuck in a few crows, and sent the picture in to join its frame. The snow scene was a great success and was sold immediately, and orders followed for more. The demand lasted until a troublesome young art student pointed out that the snow was only white paper, without even a touch of paint.

Mrs. Pimerton recalls when the New York Water Color Club came into being. Mrs. Julia Baker, Charles Warren Eaton, and Henry B. Snell thought it a good idea to have a water color exhibition during the fall, and the President of the American Water Color Society thought it undesirable. Therefore a few members of the society got together in 1890, and formed the New York Water Color Club, of which Mr. Snell was Corresponding Secretary, and Mr. Childe Hassam first President.

The first exhibition was given in November of that year in the American Art Galleries.

Mrs. Pimerton was among the first patrons, and still treasures with pride what is perhaps the only extant copy of the catalogue, a thin little leaflet containing such well-known names as Rhoda Holmes Nichols, Mrs. E. N. Scott, Ben Foster, etc.

This year it was decided to give one joint exhibition of the New York Water Color Club and American Water Color Society, and in a spirit of friendly co-operation the two boards worked together, each yielding a few points in deference to the time honored customs of the other, with the result now presented to the public.

Mrs. Pimerton is rejoiced at the combined exhibition and the revival of interest in water color painting. The little collection she possesses is her pride and joy, and she still loves her little snow scene in spite of the omniscient art student. She, by the way, was once invited to pass a few days with some intensely modern and up-to-date young people. On awaking in the morning her eyes fell upon one of the latest Cubistic productions. She thought at first that she had lost her mind, but on finding it was really a painting she hastily packed her trunk and hurried back to the companionship of her much loved water colors of long ago.

Let us hope that you too fifty years hence, when art has developed some new fashion, will still cherish a love for the water color you brought home from this exhibition."

The catalogues of the annual exhibitions of the American Water Color Society are not only a source of valuable information about the Society's exhibitions, its membership, its prizes and prize winners, but because of their numerous illustrations they constitute a record of the taste of the time by reproducing so many paintings that are now lost. These Catalogues show that many painters now better known for their oil paintings were frequent exhibitors of water colors. Among them might be mentioned Thomas Eakins, Thomas Moran, John Twachtman, J. Alden Weir, Alexander Wyant, R. Swain Gifford, Childe Hassam, and George Inness.

The early catalogues of the Society's exhibitions list a number of painters whose names are well known today. There are also a few known only to conscientious art historians. But the majority are totally unknown, and their works are scattered and almost impossible to find. Among these forgotten artists there were some who exhibited their work annually for many years.

The first annual exhibition of the American Water Color Society took place at the National Academy of Design in conjunction with their Winter Exhibition of 1867. Almost three hundred water colors were on display. As the Society flourished its exhibitions grew larger and larger until, in 1881, over eight hundred water colors were shown. Judging from its catalogues, the Society began its period of greatest affluence in 1880. In that year the catalogue was printed on large paper with many illustrations made from line drawings. As soon as the technique for making halftone illustrations from photographs was invented, the catalogues were illustrated with this new process. These illustrations form a record of the kinds of pictures that were in popular demand. In the 1880's and '90's the Society's exhibitions were very large, averaging between five and six hundred pictures each year. At this time the galleries were decorated artistically with borrowed rugs, tapestries, Tiffany vases, and old brasses. In 1887 Tiffany himself supervised the decoration of the galleries.

In his book *Art in America*, published in 1880, S. G. W. Benjamin makes this observation on the development of American interest in water color painting: "No fact better attests the active and prosperous character of American art than the rapid success which the culture of water-colors has achieved among us. In 1865 a collection of English water-color paintings was brought to this country, and exhibited in New York. It attracted much attention; and although a few artists, like Messrs. Parsons and Falconer, had already used this medium here, generally as amateurs, this seems to have been the first occasion that stimulated our artists to follow the art of water-color painting seriously.... A numerous school of artists has sprung up, finding expression wholly in water-colors, like Miss Susan Hale or Henry Farrer, the able landscape painter; while many of our leading artists in landscape and *genre* have learned ... to work with equal success in *aquarelle* and oil. The later exhibitions [of the American Water Color Society] have been characterized by an individuality and strength that compare most favorably with the exhibitions of the older societies of London."

The continuing relationship between American and British water color artists was shown in 1873 when the Society sponsored an exhibition of British water colors consisting of about two hundred pictures that were shown with the sixth annual exhibition of the Society at the National Academy of Design. In the later nineteenth century as British influence on American painting waned, new influences from the Parisian art world became more and more important. From Paris came the first hints of Japanese and other Oriental painting styles that were to exert a strong influence on all Western art, including water color painting. No less effective were the theories and techniques of the French Impressionists. And shortly after the beginning of the twentieth century, the French Moderns burst upon the scene with devastating force, dividing the American art world into two warring camps and starting the battle between artists who work in the traditional style and those who, in search of new forms and ideas, have abandoned tradition hoping to find a new freedom of expression. Since water color painting is, and always has been, based on accurate drawing, the medium does not appeal to those painters of the twentieth century who have abandoned the traditional discipline of drawing. There are still, however, many contemporary painters who value the strict discipline of basic drawing and they continue to work in traditional methods. Foremost among these are the painters in water color.

There has always been a curious reciprocal relationship between water color painting and oil painting, the technique and special effects of one medium affecting the other. However, water color developed independently of oil, and eventually the new technique of painting in water color affected the method of painting in oil colors. As the oil painting technique of the old masters was abandoned in the nineteenth century, artists began to paint directly upon white canvas without any of the preliminary steps used by the old masters. This radical change raised an argument carried on in artistic circles for many years over the relative merits of copying the "golden tone" of the older painters or trying to produce the brilliant silvery effect of water color with oil.

The effect of water color technique on oil painting is shown in a letter written by the painter Washington Allston to Thomas Sully, the portrait painter. The letter, dated 1833, reads in part: "Pray have you ever painted a picture from the water color sketch of yours which I so much admired? I mean the Mother and Child. If you have not and intend it, will you allow me to advise your copying the water color sketch as *closely as possible* as to the color. I think you will be surprised to find how *transparent* and *silvery* an *exact* imitation of it in oil will be. I am certain that Turner and perhaps also Calcot (Callcott) owe not a little of their richness of tone to the circumstance of their having commenced as painters in water color. The foil of the white paper to which their eyes were accustomed was the secret. To imitate this in oil requires not merely a high *key note*, but a powerful impasto and great clearness of tint. Should you make the experiment, let me caution you against *improving* on the sketch. If you do I venture to predict that your labor will be lost. Try to hit the precise tone, especially in the shadows."*

The application of water color technique to oil painting was to have far-reaching results in changing the style of painting in general. It was, in fact, one of the most important elements in the development of the modern art of the twentieth century.

During the nineteenth century two great controversies occupied the attention of painters in water color both in England and in America. One was over the degree of permanence of the medium and the effect of light on color fastness. Several treatises were published on the subject. The very first publication of the American Water Color Society was a pamphlet on this subject titled *Water-Color Painting. Some Facts and Authorities in Relation to its Durability* published in 1868. This pamphlet was put together by an editing committee of artists consisting of A. F. Bellows, William Hart, C. P. Cranch, J. Falconer and G. Burling, in whose studio the American Water Color Society was organized.

The other argument arose over combining opaque and transparent water color in the same picture. Although this problem now seems a matter of little consequence, it generated considerable heat and divided water color painters into two opposed camps: the purists who did not use opaque colors contemplating those who did with disdain.

Among the American water color painters of the past, few have attained the eminence of Winslow Homer (1836-1910), John LaFarge (1835-1910), John Singer Sargent (1856-1925), or the twentieth century artists Charles Demuth (1883-1935), and John Marin (1870-1953). Of these, the most famous — and the one whose fame has remained most alive — is Winslow Homer. According to a biographical note corrected by Homer himself, he was one of the founding members of the American Water Color Society in 1866.

The water color painters were one of the first groups of professional artists to organize themselves into a society — being preceded only by the architects. There seemed to be some natural cohesiveness that brought water color painters together and enabled them to carry on a flourishing organization from the very beginning. Aside from its annual exhibitions and occasional convivial gatherings of artists, the Society also serves as a center of information for those who wish to find instruction in the art, for many of its members conduct classes and give private instruction.

Since the beginning of the twentieth century, art in general has been subject to many divergent enthusiasms and influences, coming mainly from Paris. These developments of modern art have affected the ideas, attitudes, and work of many American artists in some degree. Yet through all these radical changes in the art world there has always remained a large body of painters, particularly the conservative painters in water color, who continue to use the medium in its traditional technique.

* Chamberlain Collection, Rare Book Room, Boston Public Library.

Plates

The plates are arranged in approximate chronological order. They have been selected to show the development of water color painting in America from the late eighteenth century to the present.

PLATE 1. Laurens Block. *View of New Amsterdam, 1650.* The New-York Historical Society

This is probably the first water color painted in what is now New York City. It is actually a Dutch seventeenth century work. Although it is later in date than the fantastic water colors of John White, who was in what is now Virginia in 1585, and Jacques Lemoyne, who was in the South about 1564, its realistic view of the Dutch settlement on Manhattan puts it in a different category and places it at the beginning of the history of landscape painting in water color in America.

16

PLATE 2. John Greenwood (1727-1792). *Marine View with Gibbet*. The New York Public Library

John Greenwood was born in Boston and trained as an engraver. About 1758 he went to the Netherlands, where he worked as an engraver and painted topographical landscapes and marine views in the Dutch manner, like this one. In 1762 he went to England, where he died thirty years later.

17

PLATE 3. John Singleton Copley (1738-1815). *The Ascension*. The Metropolitan Museum of Art, Purchase, Harris Brisbane Dick Fund, 1960

This pencil and wash drawing was done by Copley in Italy about 1774-1775 as a preparatory study for his large oil painting now in the Museum of Fine Arts in Boston. The subject and composition show the effect of Italian Renaissance painting on Copley's work, and the use of water color wash to give form to the figures and perspective to the landscape. The drawing has been squared off for enlargement.

PLATE 5. Eva De Peyster. *View of the Country Seat of James W. De Peyster at Bloomingdale, 1800.* The Metropolitan Museum of Art, Gift of Livingston L. Short, 1961

This picture typifies the work of the elegant lady amateur water color painter of 1800. It is a primitive documentary picture and doubtless portrays accurately, if in naive style, the actual appearance of this New York country residence. The Bloomingdale area where this house stood was in the upper West Side of Manhattan near 100th Street.

PLATE 4. John Holland (ca. 1776-1820). *Broad Street, New York, in 1797.* The
New York Public Library, I.N.P. Stokes Collection

This water color is attributed to John Holland. It is the only contemporary
view of upper Broad Street showing it as it was in the late eighteenth century.

PLATE 8. Robert Fulton (1765-1815). *Mechanical Drawing for a Steamboat*. The New York Public Library
In this drawing the artist-engineer has used water color to make a diagram of his invention.

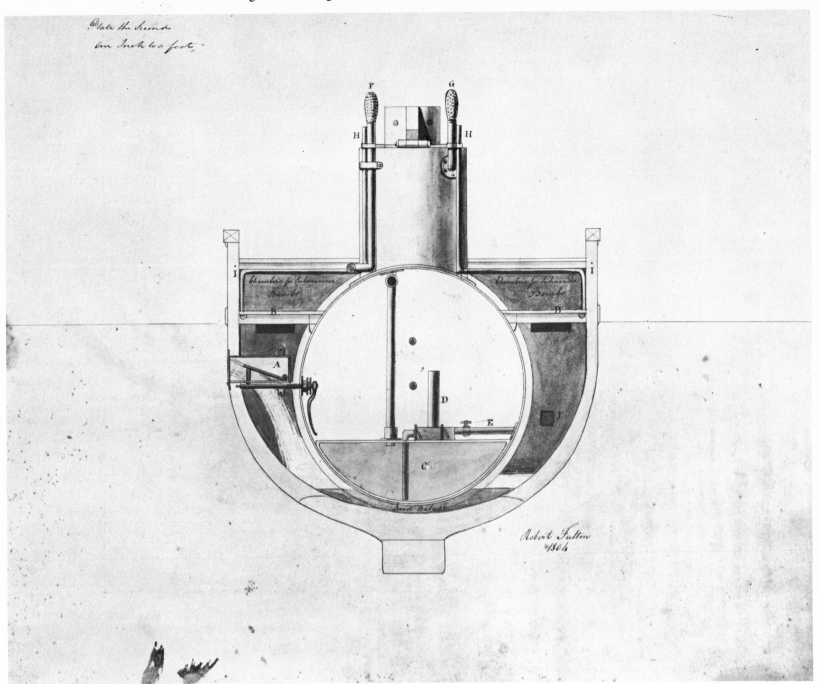

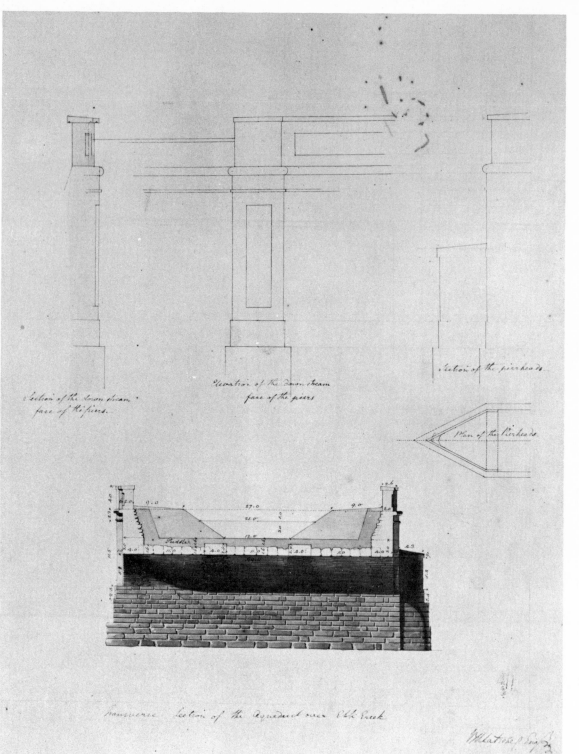

Section of the down stream
face of the piers.

Elevation of the down stream
face of the piers

Section of the pierheads

Plan of the Pierheads.

Puddle

Transverse Section of the Aqueduct over Elk Creek

PLATE 9. Benjamin Latrobe (1764-1820). *Design for a Bridge*. The New York Public Library

The architect Latrobe used water color to render a plan for an engineering project.

PLATE 10. (ca. 1815-1820). *The Water Color Class*. The Art Institute of Chicago, Gift of Emily Crane Chadbourne

Perhaps this picture records a water color class in the Robertson's Columbian Academy of Painting in New York, which they ran from about 1792 to about 1821. A box of water colors is conspicuously placed on the table at the right. Four industrious ladies are at work under the supervision of the drawing master.

PLATE 11. Charles Burton (active ca. 1802-1838). *View of the Capitol, Washington, D.C.* 1824. The Metropolitan Museum of Art, Purchase, J. Pulitzer Fund, 1942

This documentary view is the work of an immigrant British drawing master who came to the United States and worked here from about 1819 to 1842. In 1831 he published a series of views of New York and Philadelphia. Later he worked in Baltimore as a scientific draftsman. Men of this sort trained their American pupils in the British style of water color painting.

PLATE 12. William G. Wall (1792-after 1864). *View on the Hudson River.* ca. 1823. The Metropolitan Museum of Art, Edward W. C. Arnold Collection, 1954

Wall's *Hudson River Portfolio*, published in 1820, may be considered as a prime source and inspiration for the artists of the Hudson River School of American landscape painters of the early nineteenth century. Many of his views were copied by young art students and amateur water color painters.

PLATE 13. William G. Wall (1792-after 1864). *Falls of the Passaic*. The Brooklyn Museum

28

PLATE 14. John James Audubon (1785-1851). *Mourning Doves*. The New-York Historical Society

The extraordinary water color drawings made by Audubon for his famous book *Birds of America* give him a unique place in the history of American painting as well as in the history of American ornithology.

PLATE 15. John James Audubon (1785-1851). *Purple Grackle*. The New-York Historical Society

Audubon's skill as a designer and as an observer of birds in action is shown in this handsome example.

30

PLATE 16. William J. Bennett (1787-1844). *High Bridge, New York, 1844.* The New York Public Library, I.N.P. Stokes Collection

Bennett was trained in England as a print maker and water color painter. He came to New York about 1826 and painted many water color views of the streets of the city.

PLATE 17. William J. Bennett (1787-1844). *Quarantine, Staten Island*. 1833. The
Metropolitan Museum of Art, The Edward W. C. Arnold Collection, 1954

Though time has dealt harshly with this water color it still presents a lively record of shipping off the Staten Island Quarantine Station in the early nineteenth
century.

PLATE 18. John Rubens Smith (1775-1849). *Allan Melville*. The Metropolitan Museum of Art, Bequest of Charlotte E. Hoadley, 1946

Allan Melville was the father of the author Herman Melville. The portrait is described in his novel, *Pierre, or the Ambiguities*. The artist was trained in London by his father. He came to this country in 1809 and conducted drawing schools in Boston, New York, and Philadelphia.

34

PLATE 19. Thomas Birch (1779-1851). *Delaware River Front, Philadelphia.*
Museum of Fine Arts, Boston, M. and M. Karolik Collection

Thomas Birch assisted his father William in making water color drawings for the
portfolio *Views of Philadelphia*, published in 1800.

PLATE 20. William Strickland (1788-1854). *View of Ballston Spa, New York.*
ca. 1794. The New-York Historical Society

   Though Strickland is remembered principally as an architect, he made many
water color sketches during his travels in America and Europe.

36

PLATE 21. Thomas Sully (1783-1872). *Figure Studies*. Museum of Fine Arts, Boston, M. and M. Karolik Collection

It was Sully's custom to make preparatory water color sketches for his portraits to set the pose and composition before beginning to work in oil.

PLATE 22. Alexander Jackson Davis (1803-1892). *The Empire Parlour*. The New-York Historical Society   37

This drawing of an interior illustrates an architect's use of water color to show his clients how their rooms would look. Though Davis was trained as a lithographer, the greater part of his career was spent in New York as an architect. For many years he exhibited his architectural water colors at the National Academy of Design.

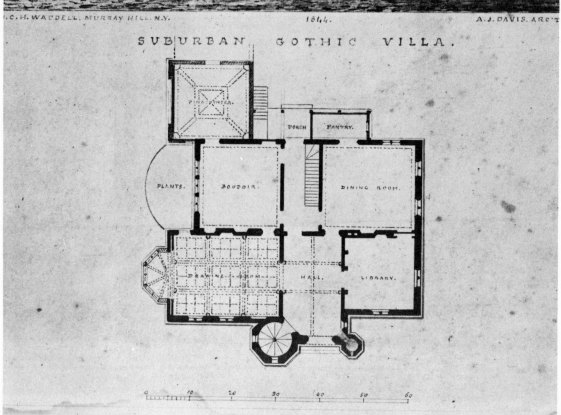

PLATE 23. Alexander Jackson Davis (1803-1892).
Suburban Gothic Villa, 1844. The New York Public Library

PLATE 24. Frances Flora Palmer (1812-1896). *The Samuel Fleet Homestead.* The Brooklyn Museum

Fanny Palmer was born and trained in England. She came to New York about 1840 and for many years was employed by the print making firm of Currier & Ives.

PLATE 25. Philip Bainbriggs (active ca. 1841). *View of Montpelier, Vermont, 1841.* The New York Public Library, I.N.P. Stokes Collection

This landscape seems to be the sole surviving work of this artist. It shows the hand of a skillful amateur, yet one not far advanced from the naive style of the primitive painter.

PLATE 27. Charles Deas (1818-1867). *The Trapper and His Family*. Museum of Fine Arts, Boston, M. and M. Karolik Collection

42

In the 1840's Charles Deas travelled in the Far West sketching the Indians and scenes of frontier life in the Indian territories.

PLATE 26. George Loring Brown (1814-1889). *Near Rome*. The Brooklyn Museum
   Brown lived for many years in Italy, where he was a very successful landscape painter.
He liked to be called "Claude" because of his admiration for the French baroque landscape
painter Claude Lorraine.

PLATE 30. John W. Hill (1812-1879). *Boston Harbor, 1856*. The New York Public Library, I.N.P. Stokes Collection

45

PLATE 31. John W. Hill (1812-1879). *Broadway and Trinity Church, 1830.*
The New York Public Library, I.N.P. Stokes Collection

46

PLATE 32. John W. Hill (1812-1879). *Bird's Nest and Flowers.* The New-York Historical Society

PLATE 33. William Ricarby Miller (1818-1893). *Self Portrait at Weehawken*.
The New-York Historical Society

This little sketch shows how the loose and rapid sketching technique of water
color prepared the way for the easy acceptance of the French Impressionist techniques that were introduced to American painters in the 1880's. Miller's landscape
views in water color, in contrast to this sketch, are highly finished in minute
detail (see Plate 34, following).

48

PLATE 34. William Ricarby Miller (1818-1893). *Catskill Clove*. 1856. The Metropolitan Museum of Art, Gift of Mrs. A. M. Miller, 1893.

This picture is typical of Miller's highly finished and detailed water color landscapes. It forms an interesting contrast to his sketchy impressionistic self-portrait.

49

PLATE 35. Felix O. C. Darley (1822-1888). *The Death of Leatherstocking*. The New York Public Library

Darley drew illustrations, reproduced as line engravings, for many books. He was best known for his illustrations for the works of Washington Irving and James Fenimore Cooper.

PLATE 36.   Mrs. A. W. Palmer (active ca. 1846). *Richard Upjohn's Studio in Trinity Church Yard*. 1846. The Metropolitan Museum of Art, The Edward W. C. Arnold Collection, 1854

Richard Upjohn was an architect whose first important commission was the Gothic Revival design for Trinity Church in New York. Nothing is known about the painter of this picture, but it appears to be the work of a talented amateur.

PLATE 37. Jasper F. Cropsey (1823-1900). *Arched Rock, Capri*. Museum of Fine Arts, Boston, M. and M. Karolik Collection

52

Cropsey was one of the founders of the American Society of Painters in Water Colors and a leading artist of the Hudson River School. He also worked as an architect and is remembered as the designer of some of the more picturesque stations on the old Sixth Avenue Elevated Railway.

PLATE 38. Ellen Robbins (1828-1905). *Flowers*. Private collection, New York

Ellen Robbins was noted as a flower painter. Most of her life was spent in Boston but in her later years she worked in St. Augustine, Florida.

PLATE 39. Samuel Colman (1832-1920). *The Green River, Wyoming*. Museum of Fine Arts, Boston, M. and M. Karolik Collection

Samuel Colman was a founder of the American Water Color Society and its first President and he showed many water colors at the Society's exhibitions. He was also a designer of furniture, textiles, and interiors in collaboration with Louis Tiffany. He made sketching trips in this country, Europe, and in North Africa. He was also considered an authority on Chinese and Japanese pottery and had a large collection of oriental art objects.

PLATE 40. Henry Van Ingen (1833-1899). *Lower Genessee Falls*. The New-York Historical Society
Van Ingen was born in Holland and came to the United States as a young man. He painted landscapes and genre scenes in water color.

PLATE 41. Wm. T. Richards (1833-1905). *A Rocky Coast*. The Metropolitan Museum of Art, Bequest of Catherine L. Wolfe, 1887

This large water color (22 x 36 inches) in its detailed geological realism shows the influence of the teachings of Ruskin on the work of the landscape and marine painters of the middle of the nineteenth century.

PLATE 42. John LaFarge (1835-1910). *Iris and Wild Roses*. The Metropolitan Museum of Art, Gift of Priscilla A. B. Henderson, 1950

LaFarge was a versatile artist working in many mediums, including stained glass. He also painted mural decorations as well as small studies of flowers.

58

PLATE 43. John LaFarge (1835-1910). *The Strange Thing Little Kiosai Saw in the River*. The Metropolitan Museum of Art, Purchase, Rogers Fund, 1917

LaFarge was one of the few American artists to travel in Japan in the later nineteenth century. The rather gruesome subject of this water color was probably inspired by a Japanese legend or fairy tale.

PLATE 44. John LaFarge (1835-1910). *Military Dance, Samoa.* The Brooklyn Museum

In his book *Reminiscences of the South Seas* the artist describes life in Samoa and the ceremonial dances with which the natives entertained him.

PLATE 45. Winslow Homer (1836-1910). *Pioneer*. The Metropolitan Museum of Art, Lazarus Fund, 1910

Homer's water colors, with their brilliantly controlled technique, their individual color harmonies, and their unhackneyed subject matter, have survived the passage of time and retained the active interest of the artist's many admirers. They have never become "dated" or of interest solely as historic documents. They seem to possess a perpetual modernity and liveliness that puts them in a very special category all their own.

In 1881 Homer went to England to stay at Tynemouth, painting the fishermen and women. At this time his water color technique had not yet developed into its final free style.

PLATE 47. Winslow Homer (1836-1910). *Channel Bass*. The Metropolitan Museum of Art, Purchase, George A. Hearn Fund, 1952

This water color records Homer's interest as a sportsman and shows his ability to design an unusual composition.

PLATE 48. Winslow Homer (1836-1910). *Flower Garden and Bungalow, Bermuda*. The Metropolitan Museum of Art, Purchase, Lazarus Fund, 1910

Homer selected this water color and those reproduced as Plates 49, 50 and 51 to represent his work in the collection of The Metropolitan Museum. In his later years he often spent the winter in the South, in Florida, in the Bahamas, and in Bermuda, where he found inspiration for many of his most famous water colors.

63

PLATE 49. Winslow Homer (1836-1910). *Palm Tree, Nassau*. The Metropolitan Museum of Art, Purchase, Lazarus Fund, 1910

PLATE 50. Winslow Homer (1836-1910). *Fishing Boats, Key West.* The Metropolitan Museum of Art, Purchase, Lazarus Fund, 1910

PLATE 51. Winslow Homer (1836-1910). *Sloop, Bermuda*. The Metropolitan Museum of Art, Purchase, Lazarus Fund, 1910

PLATE 52. Winslow Homer (1836-1910). *Fishing the Rapids*. The Brooklyn Museum

PLATE 53. Winslow Homer (1836-1910).
Homosassa River. The Brooklyn Museum

PLATE 54. Winslow Homer (1836-1910). *In the Jungle, Florida*. The Brooklyn Museum

PLATE 55. Winslow Homer (1836-1910). *Shooting the Rapids*. The Brooklyn Museum

PLATE 56. Winslow Homer (1836-1910). *The Boatman*. The Brooklyn Museum

71

PLATE 57. Winslow Homer (1836-1910). *The Turtle Pound*. The Brooklyn Museum

PLATE 58. Thomas Moran (1837-1926). *Cliffs of the Rio Virgin, Southern Utah.*
The Cooper Union Museum, New York

   Moran's reputation was based on his large canvases of western mountain scenery.
On his various trips to the West he made many water color sketches that served as
color notes and studies for his oil paintings. His style was strongly influenced by
his study of the work of Turner in England.

73

PLATE 59. Thomas Moran (1837-1926). *Looking Down from Mirror Lake, Yosemite*. The Cooper Union Museum, New York

74

PLATE 60. Thomas Moran (1837-1926).
Chicago World's Fair, 1893. The Brooklyn Museum

PLATE 61. James W. Champney (1843-1903). *Artist Sketching in a Park*. Museum of Fine Arts, Boston; M. and M. Karolik Collection

Champney was an illustrator, painter, and engraver who travelled in this country and in Europe making water color sketches. Among his better known work as an illustrator is a series of sketches showing conditions in the South ten years after the Civil War.

PLATE 62. Thomas Eakins (1844-1916). *John Biglen in a Single Scull*. The Metropolitan Museum of Art, Purchase, Fletcher Fund, 1924

Eakins' water colors, like all his works, are finished and studied with the most painstaking care. He made detailed preliminary drawings and carefully calculated perspective plans for his pictures. These studies give to his water colors an unusual degree of perfection and a sober, almost scientific, accuracy of draftsmanship and color.

76

Thomas Eakins

PLATE 63. Thomas Eakins (1844-1916). *Spinning*. The Metropolitan Museum of Art, Purchase, Fletcher Fund, 1925

PLATE 64. Thomas Eakins (1844-1916). *Negro Boy Dancing*. The Metropolitan
Museum of Art, Purchase, Fletcher Fund, 1925

PLATE 65. Thomas Eakins (1844-1916). *Cowboy Singing*. The Metropolitan Museum of Art, Purchase, Fletcher Fund, 1925

80

PLATE 66. Ralph Albert Blakelock (1847-1919).
Landscape. The Brooklyn Museum

Water colors by Blakelock are rare. This one shows
the artist in a totally different mood from that recorded in his oil paintings.

PLATE 67. Frank Boggs (1855-1926). *Along the Seine*. The Brooklyn Museum

Though Frank Boggs was an American, most of his professional life was spent in France. There he came under the influence of the Impressionists. His favorite subjects were city views and views of rivers, harbors, and beaches.

Place Bab Souika and, mosquée of Sidi Mahrez, Tunis.

Colin Campbell Cooper

PLATE 68. Colin C. Cooper (1856-1937). *Place Bab-Sanika, Tunis.* The Brooklyn Museum

  Cooper travelled and painted in Europe, North Africa, and India, but he is best known for his impressionist views of New York City.

PLATE 69. Robert Blum (1857-1903). *Street Scene in Ikao, Japan*. The Metropolitan Museum of Art, Gift of William J. Baer, 1904

Blum was known as one of the most versatile and facile draftsmen of his day. He was in Japan in 1890, where he painted many scenes of street life to illustrate his writings on Japan published in *Scribners Magazine* in 1893.

PLATE 70. John Singer Sargent (1856-1925). *Camp at Lake O'Hara*. The Metropolitan Museum of Art, Gift of Mrs. David Hecht, 1932

For Sargent his water colors were a vacation pastime, a release from the pressures and trials of constantly executing portrait commissions which forced him to consider the tastes and criticisms of his subjects, their families and friends.

PLATE 71. John Singer Sargent (1856-1925). *Mountain Stream*. The Metropolitan Museum of Art, Purchase, Pulitzer Fund, 1915

PLATE 72. John Singer Sargent (1856-1925). *Escutcheon of Charles V.* The
Metropolitan Museum of Art, Purchase, Joseph Pulitzer Fund, 1915

PLATE 73. John Singer Sargent (1856-1925). *Venetian Canal*. The Metropolitan
Museum of Art, Purchase, Pulitzer Fund, 1915

88

PLATE 74. John Singer Sargent (1856-1925). *In the Generalife, Granada*. The
Metropolitan Museum of Art, Purchase, Pulitzer Fund, 1915

PLATE 75. John Singer Sargent (1856-1925). *Spanish Fountain*. The Metropolitan Museum of Art, Purchase, Pulitzer Fund, 1915

91

PLATE 76. John Singer Sargent (1856-1925). *Santa Maria della Salute*. The Brooklyn Museum

PLATE 77. Childe Hassam (1859-1935). *Sunday Morning, Appledore*. The Brooklyn Museum

Water color sketching technique was particularly well adapted to Hassam's impressionist style of painting. His pictures with their bright colors and decorative compositional designs reflect a mood of happy contentment and pleasure in the visual beauty of nature.

PLATE 78. Childe Hassam (1859-1935). *Street in Portsmouth*. The Metropolitan Museum of Art, Purchase, Rogers Fund, 1917

94   PLATE 79. Childe Hassam (1859-1935). *The Brush House.* The Metropolitan Museum of Art, Purchase, Rogers Fund, 1917

PLATE 80. Maurice Prendergast (1859-1924). *Street Scene*. The Metropolitan
Museum of Art, Gift of the Estate of Mrs. Edward Robinson, 1952

    For Prendergast nature was merely the point of departure for the creation of
his colorful compositions. He modified his impressionistic style with its blurred
forms and accents to give his pictures something of the decorative quality of designs for tapestry or needlework.

Prendergast

PLATE 82. Maurice Prendergast (1859-1924). *Beach Scene with Boats*. The Brooklyn Museum

PLATE 81. Maurice Prendergast (1859-1924). *Piazza di San Marco*. The Metropolitan Museum of Art, Gift of the Estate of Mrs. Edward Robinson, 1952

PLATE 83. Maurice Prendergast (1859-1924). *The East River, 1901*. The Museum of Modern Art, New York

PLATE 84. Arthur B. Davies (1862-1928). *From the Quai d'Orleans*. The Brooklyn Museum

Davies is remembered today not only for his paintings but also for the important part he played in organizing the famous "Armory Show" in New York in 1913, an exhibition which caused a sensation by introducing to the American public the works of modern European painters.

99

PLATE 85. Theodore Robinson (1862-1896). *Boissise-la-Bertrand*. The Brooklyn Museum

Robinson was one of the first American artists to study the work of the French painter Monet, whose impressionist style of painting he adopted. For a time Robinson lived at Giverny in France to be near Monet and benefit by the older painter's criticism and advice.

100

PLATE 86. Frank Benson (1862-1951). *Evening*. The Metropolitan Museum of Art, Purchase, Arthur H. Hearn Fund, 1950

This picture of a flight of wild ducks coming down to alight on the water shows in the occult balance of the composition and in its free brush technique the effect of the artist's study of Chinese and Japanese paintings of birds.

102 PLATE 87. Edward Penfield (1866-1925). *Old Swedes Meeting House*. The New York Public Library
Penfield was an illustrator and designer of posters. He wrote and illustrated two books, *Holland
Sketches* and *Spanish Sketches*.

PLATE 88. William Louis Sonntag, Jr. (active ca. 1900). *Madison Square Garden*. Museum of the City of New York

These two water colors by Sonntag (Plates 88 and 89) seem to be the sole remaining record of his obscure career.

PLATE 89. William Louis Sonntag, Jr. (Active ca. 1900). *The Bowery*. 1895. Museum of the City of New York

PLATE 90. Oscar Bluemner (1867-1938). *Sun Storm*. The Museum of Modern Art, New York

Bluemner was trained in Germany as an architectural draftsman. He came to this country in 1892. The Armory Show in 1913 led him to abandon architecture for painting. His work shows, in its bright color, distorted perspective, and simplification of forms, the effect of modern European painting of the early twentieth century.

PLATE 91. Oscar Bluemner (1867-1938). *Railroad Track*. The Metropolitan Museum of Art, Bequest of Charles F. Iklé, 1963

108   PLATE 93. William Glackens (1870-1938). *Morning at Coney Island*. The Metropolitan Museum of Art, Bequest of Charles F. Iklé, 1963

Glackens impressionist style, bright color, and happy choice of subject give his pictures an enduring appeal.

PLATE 94. John Marin (1870-1953). *Pertaining to Stonington Harbor, Maine.*
The Metropolitan Museum of Art, The Alfred Stieglitz Collection, 1949

In 1946 Marin wrote, "Leave it to the true creative artist — he'll find a place for the stones and weeds of life in his picture and all so arranged that each takes its place and part in that rhythmic whole — that balanced whole — to sing its music with color, line and spacing upon its keyboard."

Marin's training as an architectural draftsman gave him an interest in structure and composition. At first the influence of Whistler is to be seen in his work, but as he matured he freely abandoned realism for a kind of ecstatic water color shorthand. With this he tried to capture essences rather than visual facts. His unique style and sense of color give his work individuality and power.

110   PLATE 95. John Marin (1870-1953). *Blue Mountain...Near Taos*. The Metropolitan Museum of Art, The Alfred Stieglitz Collection, 1949

PLATE 96. John Marin (1870-1953). *London Omnibus, 1908*. The Metropolitan
Museum of Art, The Alfred Stieglitz Collection, 1949

PLATE 97. John Marin (1870-1953). *The Old Salt.* The Metropolitan Museum of Art, The Alfred Stieglitz Collection, 1949

112

PLATE 98. John Marin (1870-1953). *Pertaining to Deer Isle — The Harbor*. The Metropolitan Museum of Art, Gift of an American, 1936

113

PLATE 99. John Marin (1870-1953). *Boats and Sea, Deer Isle, Maine*. The Metropolitan Museum of Art, The Alfred Stieglitz Collection, 1949

PLATE 100. John Marin (1870-1953). *Two-Master, Becalmed*. The Metropolitan
Museum of Art, The Alfred Stieglitz Collection, 1949

PLATE 101. Lyonel Feininger (1871-1956). *Mid-Manhattan*. The Metropolitan Museum of Art, Purchase, George A. Hearn Fund, 1953

The two principal influences affecting Feininger's paintings were his musical studies and the theories of the Cubist painters in Paris. Feininger said: "I consider my drawings and sketches as melodies, the completed painting, organized and orchestrated in color, like a large scale composition for the organ or orchestra."

PLATE 102. Arthur Dove (1880-1946). *Abstract Landscape*. The Metropolitan Museum of Art, The Alfred Stieglitz Collection, 1949

Though Dove was trained as an illustrator, his style changed after he went to Paris in 1908 and saw the work of Matisse, Kandinsky, and other painters of the Fauve group.

117

PLATE 103. Tony Sarg (1882-1942). *Barbershop*. 1919. The New York Public Library

Tony Sarg was a versatile artist turning his hand to designing, decorating, cartooning, and illustrating children's books.

118

PLATE 104. Edward Hopper (1882-   ). *House of the Fog Horn.* The Metropolitan Museum of Art, Bequest of Elizabeth A. C. Blanchard, 1956

Hopper's vision of the American city and town transforms the raw and the commonplace into severe classic beauty. His compositions are solid and spare, and they convey to the spectator the sense of isolation, solitude, and quiescence.

PLATE 105. Edward Hopper (1882-   ). *Locomotive, D. & R. G.* The Metropolitan Museum of Art, Purchase, Kastor Fund, 1957

PLATE 106. Edward Hopper (1882-   ). *The Mansard Roof*. The Brooklyn Museum

PLATE 107. Edward Hopper (1882–   ). *El Palacio*. 1946. Whitney Museum
of American Art, New York

PLATE 108. Charles Demuth (1883-1935). *Yellow and Blue*. The Metropolitan Museum of Art, The Alfred Stieglitz Collection, 1949

The water colors of Charles Demuth — particularly those of flowers — suggest by their prismatic elegance the precise, delicate opulence of pieces of jewelry.

The essence of Demuth's painting was aptly summed up in the phrase, "severe and translucent," by Melquist in his book, *The Emergence of An American Art*.

PLATE 109. Charles Demuth (1883-1935). *Roofs and Steeple*. The Brooklyn Museum

PLATE 110. Charles Demuth (1883-1935). *Stairs, Province-town.* 1920. The Museum of Modern Art, New York

125

PLATE 111. Charles Demuth (1883-1935). *Red Cabbages, Rhubarb and Orange*. The Metropolitan Museum of Art, The Alfred Stieglitz Collection, 1949

PLATE 112. Charles Demuth (1883-1935). *Flowers*. The Metropolitan Museum of Art, Purchase, Rogers Fund, 1923

PLATE 113. Charles Demuth (1883-1935). *Iris*. The Metropolitan Museum of Art, The Alfred Stieglitz Collection, 1949

PLATE 114. Charles Demuth (1883-1935). *Bermuda No. 2, The Schooner*. The
Metropolitan Museum of Art, The Alfred Stieglitz Collection, 1949

PLATE 115. Peter Arno (1904-   ). *The Parade*. The New York Public Library

130

PLATE 116. William Zorach (1887-   ). *Brooklyn Bridge*. Whitney Museum of American Art, New York

Though Zorach is best known for his work as a sculptor, his water colors show another aspect of his talent.

PLATE 117. Georgia O'Keefe (1887-   ). *Evening Star III*. 1917. The Museum
of Modern Art, New York

132

   Georgia O'Keefe's work in water color and in oil shows her powerful, individual
feeling for color and design.

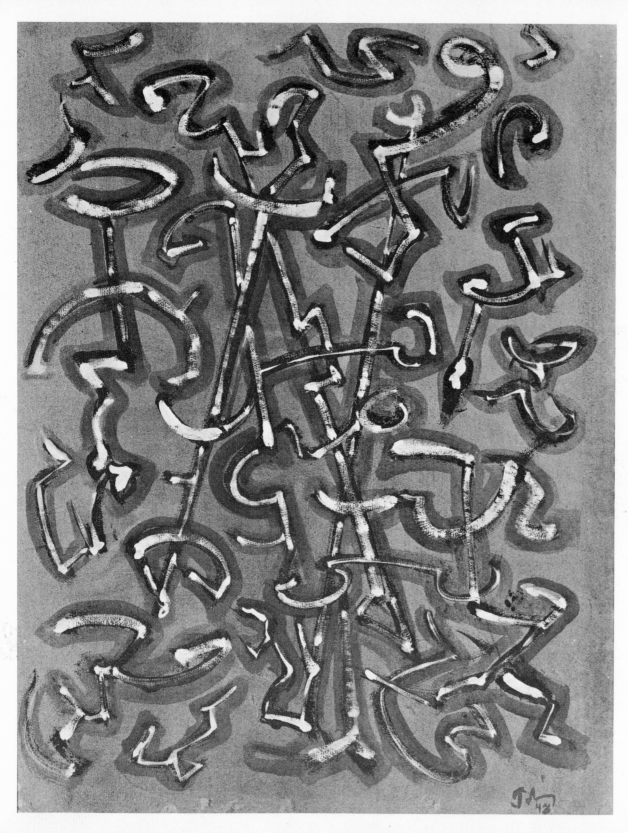

PLATE 119. Mark Tobey (1890-   ). *Transit*. The Metropolitan Museum of Art, Purchase, George A. Hearn Fund, 1949

The "white writing" of Tobey's paintings is related to Japanese calligraphy, an esoteric art in which design and meaning combine into abstraction.

PLATE 120. Eliot O'Hara (1890-   ). *Noon-day Glare*. The Brooklyn Museum

O'Hara's reputation is based not only on his water colors but also on his work as a teacher and as the author of many books on water color technique.

PLATE 121. Charles Burchfield (1893-   ). *The Coming of Spring*. The Metropolitan Museum of Art, Purchase, George A. Hearn Fund, 1943

Burchfield himself said of this picture: "The attempt here was to express . . . the contrast of winter and spring by showing two kinds of hollows or ravines. . . . One was to be dead and lifeless . . . the other to be alive with growing things."

This imaginary landscape is painted in the abstract and stylized manner of his later work.

PLATE 122. Charles Burchfield (1893-   ). *The False Front*. The Metropolitan
Museum of Art, Purchase, Rogers Fund, 1924

    Burchfield, in his earlier work, found beauty and interest in the grim, ram-
shackle Victorian structures in rural areas and small towns.

138 PLATE 123. Charles Burchfield (1893-   ). *August Afternoon.* The Metropolitan Museum of Art, Purchase, Morris K. Jesup Fund, 1928

PLATE 124. Charles Burchfield (1893-   ). *Dandelion Seed-Ball and Trees*. The Metropolitan Museum of Art, Purchase, Arthur H. Hearn Fund, 1940

PLATE 125. Stuart Davis (1894-1964). *Iris*. The Metropolitan Museum of Art, Purchase, George A. Hearn Fund, 1948

Although Stuart Davis was a pupil of Robert Henri, he early abandoned realistic painting for abstractions done in patterns of bright flat color with strong accents of black. This example of his work is done in opaque water color.

PLATE 126. Nicolai Cikovsky (1894-   ). *Light*. The Brooklyn Museum

In this picture the elements of landscape are simplified to nearly complete abstraction.

PLATE 127. Adolf Dehn (1895-   ). *Sea and Rocks*. The Brooklyn Museum
Dehn's water color landscapes, painted in all parts of the country, make a pleasing and lively record of his extensive travels.

PLATE 128. Reginald Marsh (1898-1954). *Coney Island Beach, Number 1*. 1943.
Whitney Museum of American Art, New York

143

Reginald Marsh found his subjects on the crowded beaches and in the amusement parks and slum streets of New York. These he has recorded with a sort of brutal baroque ferocity bordering on caricature.

PLATE 129. Reginald Marsh (1898-1954). *Locomotive In Weehawken*. The Brooklyn Museum

PLATE 130. Alexander Calder (1898-   ). *Composition*. 1953. Whitney Museum of American Art, New York, Gift of Mrs. Milton Weill

145

Though Calder is better known for his mobile and stabile sculpture, his drawings and water colors show the same kind of arresting quality of design and color.

146   **PLATE 131. John Whorf (1903-1959).** *Southern Ocean.* **The Metropolitan Museum of Art, Purchase, George A. Hearn Fund, 1939**

Whorf once said, "I am not a marine painter or a landscape painter or a portrait painter; I am a water color painter."

PLATE 132. Mario Cooper (1905-   ). *Houseboat, Tokyo Canal*. The Metropolitan Museum of Art, Gift of Mrs. Robert J. Meyers, 1963

Cooper has traveled extensively in the Far East and recorded his journeys in a series of water colors that show the influence of the art of the orient.

PLATE 133. Ogden Pleissner (1905-   ). *Along the Arno*. The Metropolitan Museum of Art, Purchase, George A. Hearn Fund, 1946

In Pleissner's work something of the painter's pleasure in his facile and controlled handling of water color is communicated to the viewer.

PLATE 134. Ogden Pleissner (1905-   ). *The Shrine*. The Metropolitan Museum of Art, Purchase, Hugo Kastor Fund, 1962

PLATE 135. William Thon (1906-   ). *Quarry*. The Brooklyn Museum
William Thon, a self-taught painter, is especially noted for his dramatic and
original interpretations of landscape.

PLATE 136. Kenneth Callahan (1906-   ). *Conversation*. The Brooklyn Museum

Callahan believes that Nature is the most important, the initial source of inspiration in art. His work shows the effect of his study of the brush work of the Chinese and Japanese landscape painters of the past.

151

152

PLATE 137. Henry Gasser (1909-   ). *The Black Bridge.* The Metropolitan Museum of Art, Gift of Mr. and Mrs. J. A. Robb, 1960

Henry Gasser as artist, teacher, and author demonstrates his firm command of water color technique.

PLATE 138. Morris Graves (1910-   ). *Spirit Bird Transporting Minnow from Stream to Stream*. The Metropolitan Museum of Art, Purchase, Arthur H. Hearn Fund, 1954

The unique imagination of Morris Graves and his study of oriental art give to his work a tantalizing mystical character that is rarely found in modern painting.

153

154

PLATE 139. Dong Kingman (1911-). *The "El" and Snow*. Whitney Museum of American Art, New York

Though Dong Kingman was born in California, he was educated in China and first learned to paint there. This accounts for much of his free brush style.

PLATE 140. Bill Bomar (1919-   ). *White Island*. The Brooklyn Museum

Bill Bomar, a Texas painter, was trained at the Cranbrook Academy of Art and also studied with John Sloan and Amédée Ozenfant.

PLATE 141. Jacob Armstead Lawrence (1917-   ). *Tombstones*. 1942. Whitney Museum of American Art, New York

Lawrence says "My work is abstract in the sense of having been designed and composed, but it is not abstract in the sense of having no human content."

PLATE 142. Lloyd Lózes Goff (1917-). *Texas Oil Fire*. 1938. Whitney Museum of American Art, New York

In this picture water color is used to record the landscape with an almost photographic realism.

157

158

PLATE 143. Andrew Wyeth (1917-). *Island Beacon*. The Metropolitan Museum of Art, Purchase, George A. Hearn Fund, 1946

The message of the beacon, though it is evidence of an attempt at communication, is the anguish of loneliness, an emotion conveyed in this painting by both color and composition.

PLATE 144. Sam Francis (1923-   ). *Structure No. 2.*
The Metropolitan Museum of Art, The Edward Joseph
Gallagher Memorial Collection, 1958

In this water color all traditional subject, drawing, and
composition are abandoned in order to emphasize the effect
of a pure color structure.

List of Plates (Page numbers in bold face indicate Color Plates.)